EGINNING

PIANO

SOLO

en

GREATEST STANDARDS

ARRANGED BY GARY MEISNER

D0752125

ISBN 1-4234-0092-5

HAL•LEONARD®
CORPORATION

7777 W. BLUEMOUND RD. P.O. BOX 13819 MILWAUKEE, WI 53213

Visit Hal Leonard Online at
www.halleonard.com

All The Things You Are

from VERY WARM FOR MAY

Lyrics by OSCAR HAMMERSTEIN II
Music by JEROME KERN

Moderately

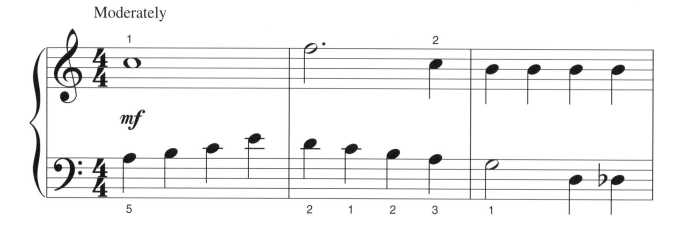

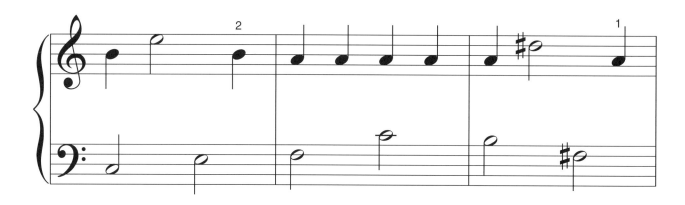

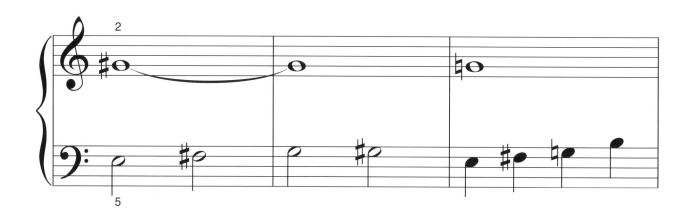

1   4

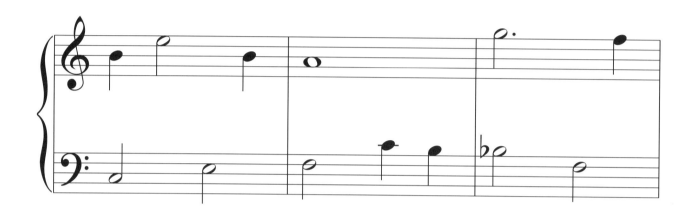

BLUE SKIES

from BETSY

Words and Music by
IRVING BERLIN

Moderately

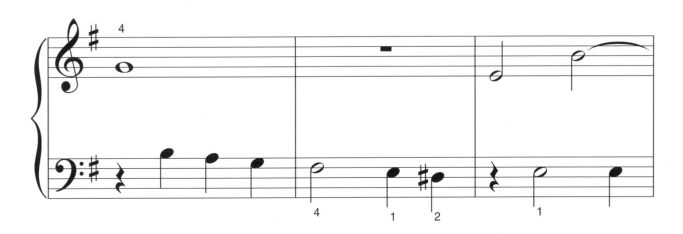

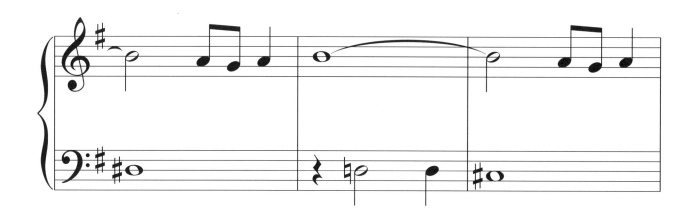

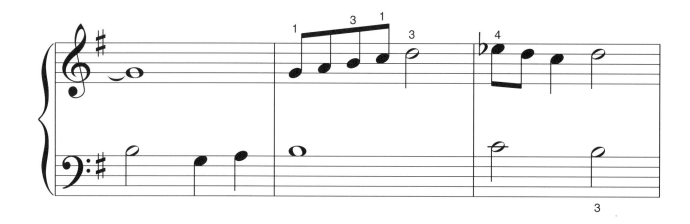

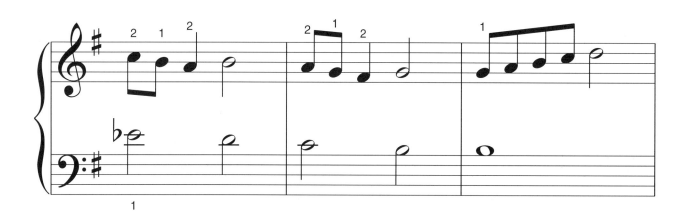

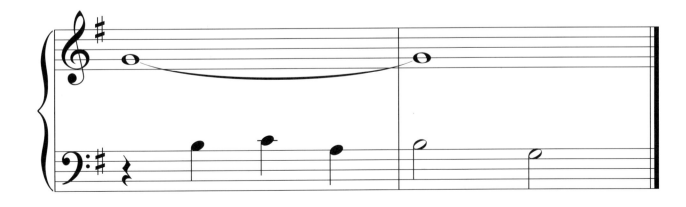

8

AUTUMN LEAVES

English lyric by JOHNNY MERCER
French lyric by JACQUES PREVERT
Music by JOSEPH KOSMA

Moderately

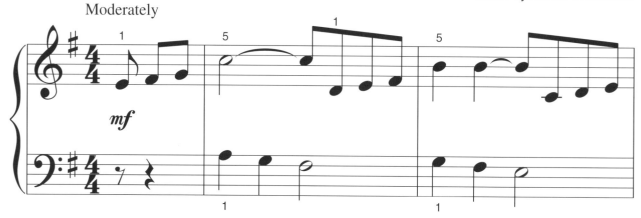

© 1947, 1950 (Renewed) ENOCH ET CIE
This arrangement © 2005 ENOCH ET CIE
Sole Selling Agent for U.S. and Canada: MORLEY MUSIC CO., by agreement with ENOCH ET CIE
All Rights Reserved

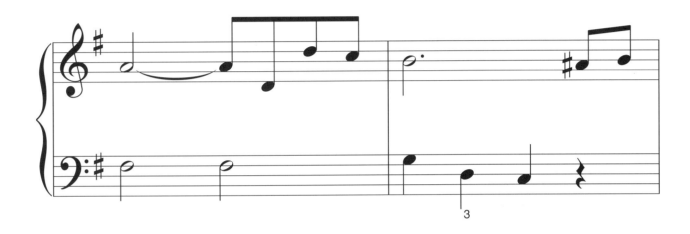

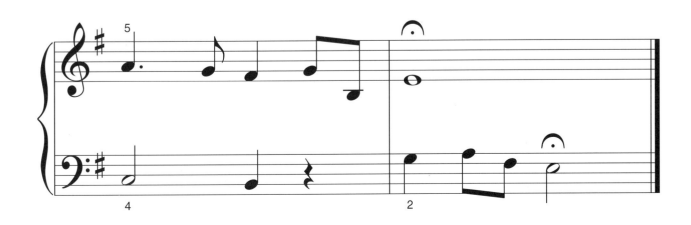

MOON RIVER
from the Paramount Picture BREAKFAST AT TIFFANY'S

Words by JOHNNY MERCER
Music by HENRY MANCINI

Slowly

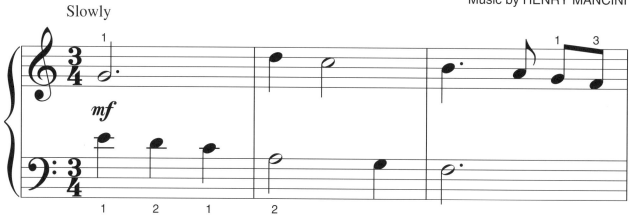

12

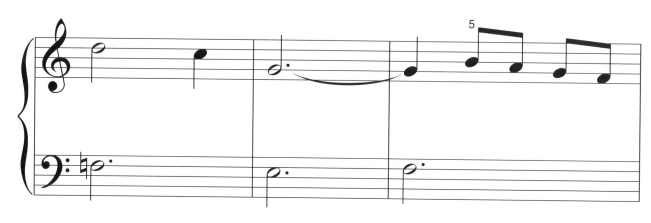

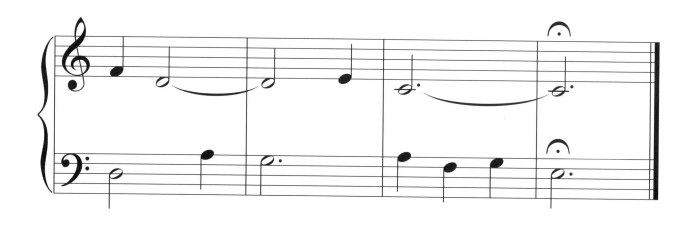

THE NEARNESS OF YOU

from the Paramount Picture ROMANCE IN THE DARK

Words by NED WASHINGTON
Music by HOAGY CARMICHAEL

Slowly

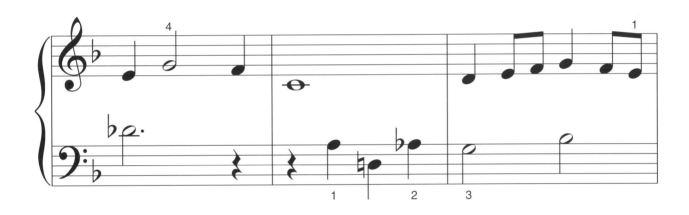

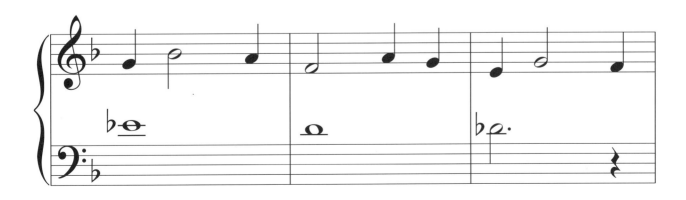

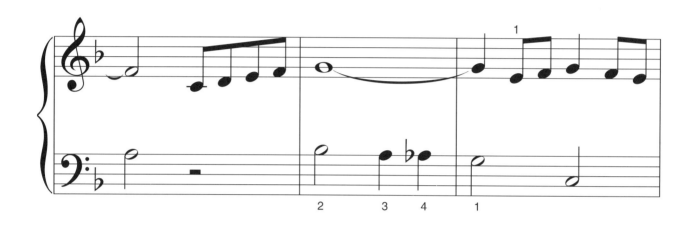

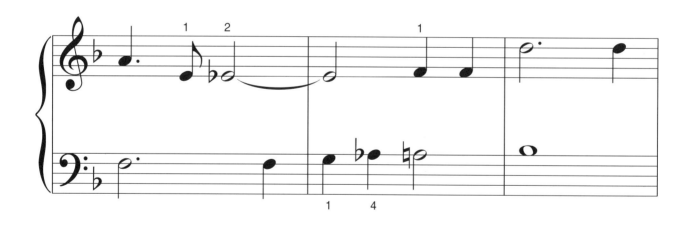

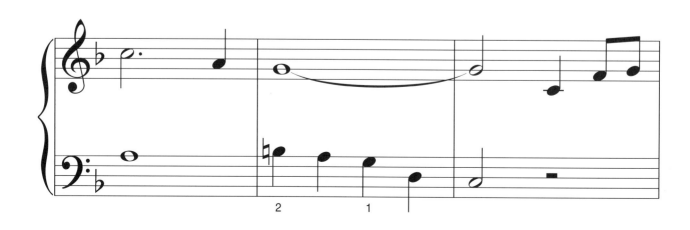

STELLA BY STARLIGHT
from the Paramount Picture THE UNINVITED

Words by NED WASHINGTON
Music by VICTOR YOUNG

Moderately

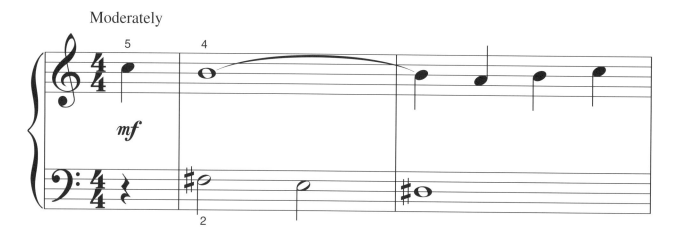

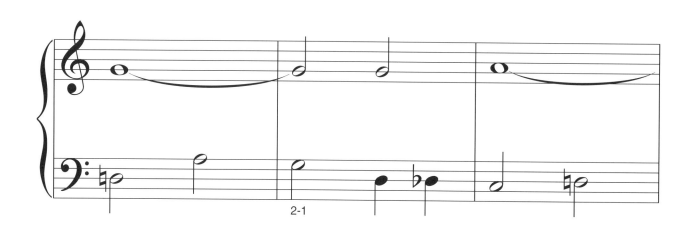

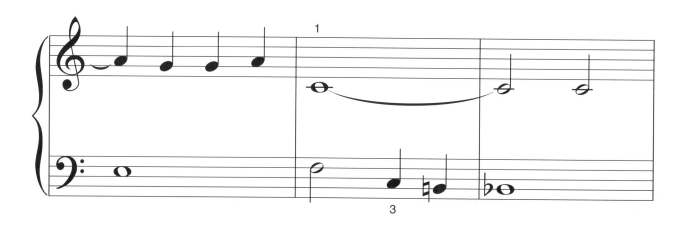

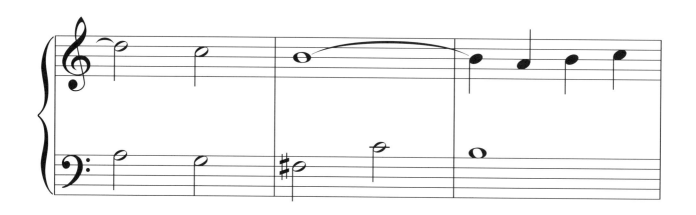

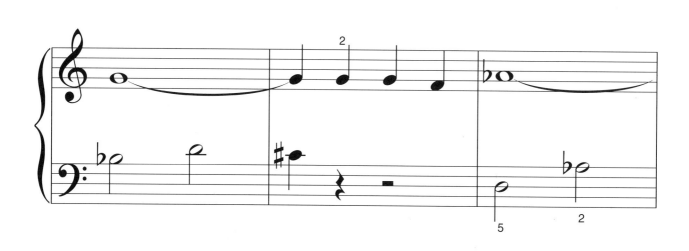

WHAT A WONDERFUL WORLD

Words and Music by GEORGE DAVID WEISS
and BOB THIELE

Slowly

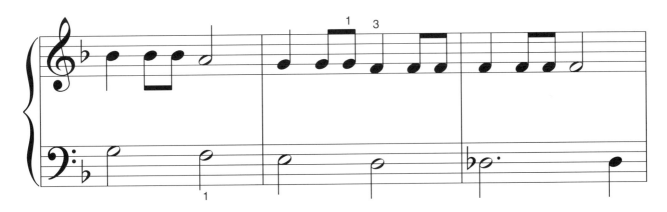

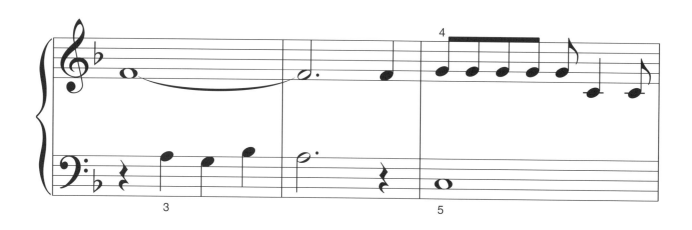

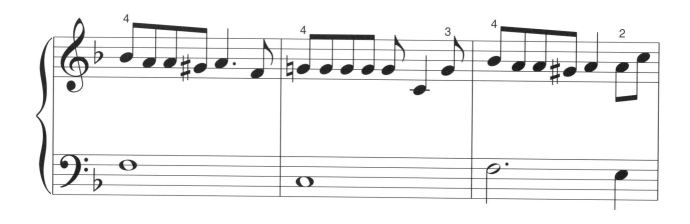

The Way You Look Tonight

from SWING TIME

Words by DOROTHY FIELDS
Music by JEROME KERN

Moderately

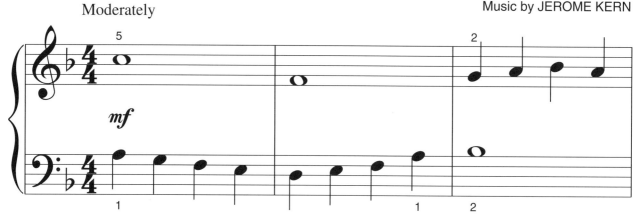

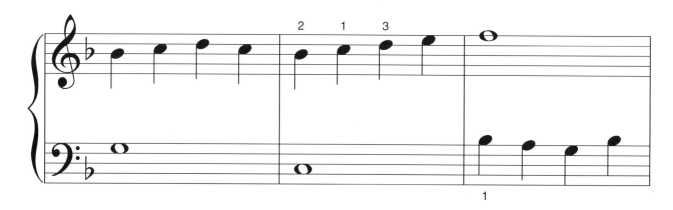

To Coda ⊕

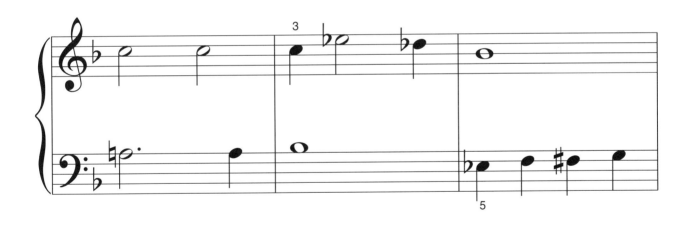

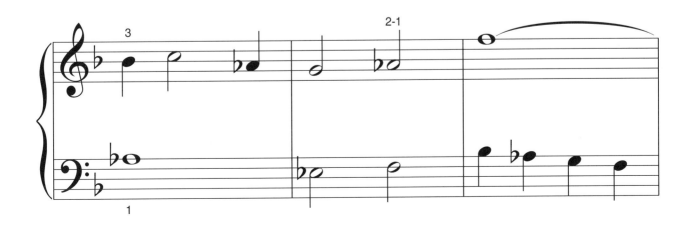

D.C. al Coda

CODA